SNAKES SMELL WITH THEIR TONGUES!

AND OTHER AMAZING FACTS

By Thea Feldman
Illustrated by Lee Cosgrove

Ready-to-Read

SIMON SPOTLIGHT

An imprint of Simon & Schuster Children's Publishing Division • New York London Toronto Sydney New Delhi
1230 Avenue of the Americas, New York, New York 10020 • This Simon Spotlight edition July 2021 • Copyright © 2021 by
Simon & Schuster, Inc. Stock photos by iStock. All rights reserved, including the right of reproduction in whole or in part
in any form. SIMON SPOTLIGHT, READY-TO-READ, and colophon are registered trademarks of Simon & Schuster, Inc. For
information about special discounts for bulk purchases, please contact
Simon & Schuster Special Sales at 1-866-506-1949 or business@simonandschuster.com.
Manufactured in the United States of America 0621 LAK
2 4 6 8 10 9 7 5 3 1
CIP data is available from the Library of Congress.
ISBN 978-1-5344-8522-8 (hc)
ISBN 978-1-5344-8521-1 (pbk)
ISBN 978-1-5344-8523-5 (eBook)

GLOSSARY

cold-blooded: having a body temperature that matches the temperature of its surroundings

constrictor: a snake that coils around its prey and squeezes it to death

habitat: a place where an animal lives in nature

ligament: a tough band of tissue that connects one bone to another

predator: an animal that hunts, kills, and eats other animals

prey: an animal hunted by a predator for food

reptile: a cold-blooded animal whose body is usually covered in scales or bony plates

shed: to grow out of and lose, such as an outgrown skin

species: a specific kind of animal or plant

venom: a type of poison that one animal injects into another animal

Note to readers: Some of these words may have more than one definition. The definitions above match how these words are used in this book.

CONTENTS

Did you know that some snakes climb trees and that others swim, or glide through the air?

Did you know that snakes hear with their jawbones and smell with their tongues?

By the time you finish this book, you'll know all about what makes snakes so sssssuper!

CHAPTER 1

SO MANY SNAKES!

There are more than three thousand species (say: SPEE-shees), or kinds, of snakes.

The red diamond rattlesnake lives in the Southern California mountains and deserts, and on some islands.

NORTH AMERICA

SOUTH AMERICA

The yellow-bellied sea snake swims in the open ocean.

They live in most types of habitats (say: HAB-eh-TATS), from warm, tropical places to deserts—and oceans.

The European common adder is the only European snake to live in below-freezing temperatures!

ARCTIC CIRCLE

EUROPE

ASIA

AFRICA

EQUATOR

The king cobra is found in rain forests, including those in India.

AUSTRALIA

ANTARCTICA

Snakes come in all different sizes, colors, and patterns too. They are commonly divided into two categories: ones with venom and ones without.

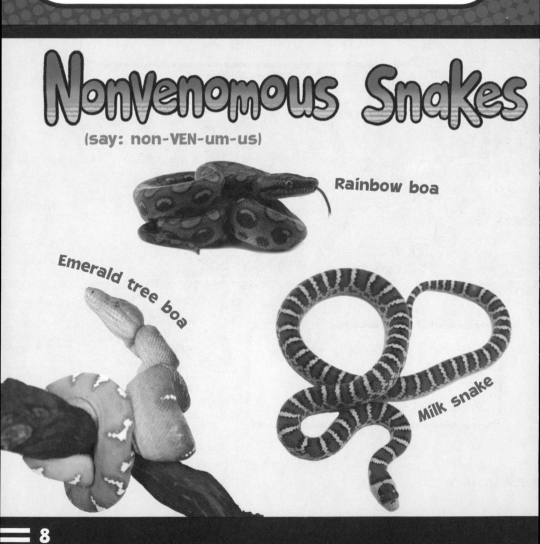

Nonvenomous Snakes

(say: non-VEN-um-us)

Rainbow boa

Emerald tree boa

Milk snake

Venom (say: VEN-um) is a poison that one animal injects into another animal.

Venomous Snakes

king cobra

copperhead

Inland taipan

The coral snake has bright colors to warn other animals to steer clear!

A venomous snake bites its prey (say: PRAY) and, through its fangs, injects the prey with venom. The venom stuns or kills the prey.

All snakes are reptiles (say: REP-tyles). They have scaly skin and are cold-blooded animals that lie in the sun to get warm, and go into the shade or the water to keep cool.

A snake's pattern can help it blend into its surroundings. Can you see the eastern diamondback rattlesnake?

CHAPTER 2

HISS AND TELL

A snake keeps growing for its entire life. But its skin doesn't!

Right before it sheds its skin, a snake's eyes turn milky blue!

So a snake sheds or loses its skin several times a year.

A snake slithers out of its old skin headfirst.

Ahh! Much better!

A snake rubs against something to help shed its old skin.

Snakes range in size from four inches to over twenty feet! A reticulated (say: rah-TIC-you-LAY-ted) python can be up to 32 feet long—over 90 times longer than the Barbados (say: bar-BAY-dose) threadsnake!

Heavyweight champion! An anaconda
(say: AN-a-CON-da) can weigh up to 550 pounds!

Flick! A snake moves its tongue through the air. The tongue picks up tiny amounts of odors from the snake's surroundings and carries them to the roof of the snake's mouth. And that's how a snake smells things!

A snake manages to hear through the bones in its lower jaw. The bones pick up vibrations of moving things and send messages about them to the snake's brain.

Those are some good vibrations!

Snakes have no external ears!

All snakes are predators
(say: PRED-uh-ters) that hunt
and eat prey.
Some snakes grab prey with their
teeth and swallow the prey alive.

The king cobra eats small
animals but has enough venom
to kill an elephant!

Other snakes are constrictors (say: cun-STRICT-ers). A constrictor grabs prey and wraps its body around the animal. The constrictor restricts their prey's blood flow until it dies, and then eats it.

Boas and other constrictors squeeze their prey to death, but no bones get broken!

All snakes' teeth face inward and keep prey from being able to escape.

All snakes swallow their prey whole. And thanks to ligaments (say: LIG-uh-mints)—which are tough bands of tissue—in the jaw that s-t-r-e-t-c-h, a snake can swallow prey three times larger than its head!

The bigger the snake, the bigger the meal it can swallow. A python regularly eats about one quarter of its body weight at once, but sometimes swallows things larger than itself!

Want to eat as much as a python? You'll have to chow down on **240** quarter-pound cheeseburgers!

CHAPTER 3

THAT'S REALLY MOVING!

The black mamba has been clocked speeding along at twelve and a half miles per hour. That may not seem terribly fast, but it's pretty impressive for someone with no legs!

Man: up to 27.8 miles per hour

0 mph | 5 mph | 10 mph | mph | 25 mph | 30

Black mamba: up to 12.5 miles per hour

Blink and you've missed it. What? In the amount of time it takes a person to blink once, a western diamondback rattlesnake can strike at prey four times!

Golden flying snake

Paradise tree snake

Banded flying snake

Moluccan flying snake

Indian flying snake

Some snakes live mostly in trees, and when they need to move, they just glide through the air!

To glide through the air, a snake flattens its ribs into a C shape and then moves its body in S-shaped waves.

Other snakes live in the sea, where their oar-like tails help them swim!

A sea snake dives to the seafloor to find food.

Say what? Some scientists believe that snakes have friends!

Studies of eastern garter snakes show that they look for other snakes to hang out with—and are picky about it!

If you could be a snake, would you like to move on land, through the air, or in water?

Would you like to smell things with your tongue and hear things with your jaw?

There are so many awesome things about snakes! What is your favorite thing that a snake can do?

Turn the page to learn some more very surprising facts about snakes!

There are about six hundred species of venomous snakes in the world, of which about two hundred can kill or seriously hurt humans. But scientists also know that snake venom can be made into medicines that can save or help human lives!

Since 1981, venom from the Brazilian pit viper has been used in a blood pressure medicine that is commonly prescribed worldwide. Two medicines based on snake venom that help treat heart conditions were approved in the late 1990s. And now scientists are studying how snake venom may be used in even more medicines. One team is working with king cobra venom to see

how it might be developed into an effective painkiller. More than one hundred other snake venoms, including that of the Iranian spider-tailed viper, are also being studied to see how they might help stop dangerous blood clots. Snakes are not just super—some can be *super*heroes!